S0-BRN-631

GIFTS
FOR PERSONAL
GROWTH AND
RECOVERY

Wayne Kritsberg

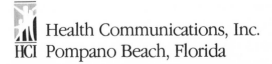
Health Communications, Inc.
Pompano Beach, Florida

Wayne Kritsberg
Austin, Texas

Cover design by Vicki Sommer

Library of Congress Cataloging-in-Publication Data

Kritsberg, Wayne, 1942-
    Gifts for personal growth.

    Bibliography: p.
    1. Self-realization. 2. Alcoholism — Treatment.
3. Mind and body. 4. Therapeutics, Physiological.
I. Title.
BF637.S4K75   1987   616.86'106   87-21196
ISBN 0-932194-60-5

© 1988 Wayne Kritsberg
   ISBN 0-932194-60-5

All rights reserved. No part of this book may be reproduced or transmitted in any form or by any means, electronic or mechanical, including photocopying, recording, or by an information retrieval system without permission in writing from the publisher.

Printed in the United States of America

Published by: Health Communications, Inc.
               1721 Blount Road
               Pompano Beach, FL 33069

The personal examples used in this book are based on my experiences as a counselor. In all cases involving quotations from client histories, I have either used composites of several different people, or changed the clients' names. This was done to ensure privacy and confidentiality.

Acknowledgments

There were many people who encouraged me to write this book, and who have given me encouragement during the actual process of writing it. To all these people I wish to express my deepest appreciation and thanks; without their support this project would have been much more difficult. There are, however, four people who I wish to acknowledge for their special contributions to this endeavor:

Jan Sargent: For her artwork.

Annemarie Micklo: Her many hours of editorial guidance are but a small part of her contribution to this book. Her love, encouragement, ideas, and hard work made this book happen.

Marie Stilkind: The editorial decisions she made, and vision she had about how to improve and expand this book, did much to make this book what it is.

Ceci Miller-Kritsberg: Her editorial expertise and creative ideas contributed a depth and clarity to the final draft of this work that otherwise would have been missing. Her loving support and hard work helped to make this book possible.

Thank you very much.

Dedication

I dedicate this book to all of those who have shared themselves with me and who, in their turn, have allowed me to share myself with them.

Author's Note

This book focuses both on those recovering from Alcoholism and Chemical Dependency and on adult children of alcoholics and some of the difficulties they have as a result of growing up in an alcoholic family. It is important to understand that the alcoholic family is only one type of dysfunctional family system, and that all dysfunctional families follow the same general family rules (denial, rigidity, silence and isolation). Any person who comes from a dysfunctional family, alcoholic or otherwise, will be referred to here as an "adult child". If you did not come from an alcoholic family, but came from some other kind of dysfunctional family system, these rules apply to you, too, and so do the solutions.

Contents

Introduction

There is a power in each one of us that heals. We are born with this power; it is our birthright as human beings. This healing power is not normally accessible to us. Somehow, as we move through the day-to-day process of our lives, we lose the knowledge that we have the gift of self-healing. For whatever reason, we repress our birthright of self-healing.

The purpose of this book is to assist you back to an awareness of your own healing power. It is to give you the tools and the space so that you can begin the process of healing the wounds and pain of addictive behavior and of growing up in an alcoholic or other dysfunctional family system.

The techniques in this book can be effectively used to accelerate and enhance your growth and healing. For the person who is recovering from alcoholism or other chemical addictions these techniques are most effective after you have been alcohol and drug-free for a period of time. This period of time can only be determined by the individual, and will be different for each person. If you are recovering in a 12-step program, such as A.A., these tools are not intended to replace that program.

Many people who read this book will not be chemically dependent, but will have been raised in alcoholic or other dysfunctional family systems. The tools in this book are designed to be used by you also. The pain and wounds of being the child of a dysfunctional family system go deep. If you are in a 12-step recovery program, I strongly encourage you to continue to work that program. Use the tools in this book to enhance that program, not to replace it.

The techniques described in this book are tools you can use in the day-to-day process of living. These tools are powerful and they do work. The beauty of them is that once you learn to use them, you have them at your disposal for the rest of your life.

There is an old Chinese proverb that goes:

Give a man a fish and you feed him for a day.
Teach a man to fish and you feed him for a life-
time.

This is what these tools are all about.

This is truly a gift.

1

The
Personal Journal

Deep within each one of us is a well of information and experience that is not normally accessible. It is important to an individual's process of personal development and growth that this hidden information and experience become available. Writing in a personal journal is a powerful method for the individual to gain access to the inner resources and experiences that are a necessary part of self-discovery and growth. In this section we will discuss how to set up and use a personal journal and how this journal can be used effectively.

The journal that I will be discussing is not a diary, nor is it just a record of what has happened and how we feel about our experiences. The personal journal, when used correctly, becomes an instrument that takes the writer on a journey into the inner landscape of his being. This journey is never really completed. The traveler resolves various conflicts in his life and discovers that as his life unfolds, he is constantly realizing new and more important insights.

Two of the advantages of the journal process are that not only do insights occur, but the journal also provides an arena where past and present conflicts can be resolved.

A person who is using a journal can explore as deeply into his life as he wishes; he can also move as fast or as slowly as he wishes. The journal is a self-paced and self-governing medium.

The personal journal is not a substitute for the 4th step inventory found in 12-step programs, such as A.A., N.A. and Al-Anon.

There are many ways of keeping a journal, and there are many styles and structures that can be adopted. I feel that it is important to allow the journal to grow of its own accord. Each person's journal is a reflection of his own inner experiences and therefore is unique. The following are guidelines that I use when setting up a personal journal.

Journal Sections

A fundamental aspect of the journal is that it is divided into sections, with dividers. Journal entries are made in the different sections of the journal. As the person grows, so does the journal. Every time we make a new section, we add a divider and write the heading of the section on the tab on the divider. This allows easy identification of the various journal sections.

It has been my experience that keeping the journal in a three-ring, looseleaf notebook is the most flexible and practical method. The personal journal is not a linear document, but an open-ended process. As we use the journal, we will be moving from one section to another and adding material to different sections. A looseleaf notebook allows the journal to grow.

Every time an entry is made in the journal, it should be dated. This is very important because it helps the writer position himself in the movement of his life. Without a sense of when something occurred, an individual can easily become confused, and this confusion can distort memories. In many instances, it is also advisable to note the time of the day.

The following are the sections that I have found the most useful for the beginning journal writer. In the following examples I have used the journal entries of a former client of mine named Mary.

Daily Entries

This section is similar to a diary. Here we record the events of our lives as they happen, and record how we feel about these events. For instance:

12/7/82

I talked to my ex-husband John today. I had the same old feeling of anger and frustration that I generally get when I talk to him.

It is important to commit to making daily entries on a regular basis for at least a month. This helps you get a feel for the journal and become accustomed to using it.

Personal History

Each of us has a personal history that is unique. It is this personal history that sets us apart from each other and from our closest family members. Even identical twins who were raised together have separate and distinct histories.

In this section of the journal, we record the events and experiences that make up our personal history. Much of the future work that will be done in the personal journal comes from the information in this section. It is here, in the personal history section, that we identify the experiences that have helped to shape and direct our lives.

The alcoholic or the adult child from an alcoholic family has, in many instances, no sense of the continuity of his life. As a result of repressing painful emotional experiences, he often has large chunks of time missing from his childhood memories. He may also have memories that are distorted because a situation is too painful to remember as it really happened, or the situation is remembered through an alcoholic haze. By using the personal history section, the person can re-establish a knowledge of, and a feeling for, his or her past.

Like the daily entries section, the personal history section is established by using a divider. The title on the tab of the divider is "Personal History."

To start this section, list ten or twelve of the major events of your life (remember to date the entry). These events, or milestones, are the markers that have helped to shape your life. It is important to keep this list of milestones to a manageable length, no more than a dozen events should be picked.

6

The following example is a list of Mary's milestones:

12/7/82

I was born.
I got sober.
I got married to John.
I went to college.
I did my 4th-step inventory.
I was divorced.
I lost my job because of alcohol.
I moved to the Midwest.
I experienced God in my life.
My dad died of alcoholism.
I left the church.
I gave birth to my child.

It is not necessary that the list be in chronological order. What is important is that you become aware of the events themselves, not their sequence.

When the list is complete, at your leisure, write about each of the milestones in detail. As you explore each event, you will gain a new sense of awareness and new perspectives about your life. It is not necessary to write at great length about these milestones; many times a page or even a paragraph will be enough.

There will, however, be times when you become aware that what you are writing about is causing emotional pain, that the issues you are examining are not resolved. When this happens you can often resolve these hidden issues by continuing to write about them in further detail, or by working through them with a counselor.

In the personal history section, I would also suggest that you make a list of the important persons in your life.

This list can contain persons who are currently active in your life, or persons who are, for one reason or another, no longer a part of your day-to-day life.

Mary's list was:

Dad
Mom
Harry (my son)
John (my ex-husband)
Karen (my friend)
Tom (my brother)
Sandy (my sister)

Each of the important people in your life should have his or her own section in the personal journal. In these sections record how you feel about the relationship that you have with that person. I will continue to use Mary as an example.

Mary's ex-husband, John, was on her list of important people, and she also made entries in the daily entries section about him. It would be important, therefore, for Mary to have a section in her journal exclusively for John. In this section she would explore in depth her relationship with her ex-husband and resolve some of the conflict that continues to be a part of that relationship.

Dialoguing

In order for Mary to work in her journal with her ex-husband in a meaningful way, she can use a technique called dialoguing. Dialoguing is the process of having a conversation, which is written down on paper, with another person, who is not present. During this conversation or dialogue, the person who is writing enters into a dialogue with the other person as if that person were present. As the dialogue progresses, the interaction between the two parties will become more and more spontaneous. As this process unfolds, the answers that the writer of the dialogue gets from the person with whom he is dialoguing can be very important in resolving issues that are blocking the growth of the relationship.

To break the ice in this conversation, Mary would first write a statement in the section about John, focusing on where their relationship is now. This focusing statement is short and to the point. Example:

12/8/82

> *Even though John and I have been divorced for almost two years, I still feel a lot of anger whenever I talk to him. But we have to talk; we see each other at A.A. meetings and we share custody of our son, Harry.*

Next, Mary makes a list of the major events in John's life, the milestones that have shaped his life. They should be done in the first person, as if John were listing them himself. Example:

I was born on 11/2/39.
My father was an alcoholic.
My mother died when I was 13.
I left school to join the Navy.
I got married to Mary.
I had a son, Harry.
I got sober.
I was divorced.
I was remarried to June.

The purpose of the above list is to help Mary get a feel for how John's life has been. It is not necessary for Mary to make a new list each time she dialogues with John; she should, however, review the list of his milestones each time she dialogues with him and update it occasionally.

At this point Mary would be ready to begin to dialogue with John. Dialoguing is a lot like writing a script for a play, except that one allows the dialogue to flow freely and spontaneously, not trying to control or edit it. Example:

Mary: Hello, John.
John: Hi.
Mary: I think that this is foolish.
John: That's OK.
Mary: I get so mad at you.
John: I know you do, but you never tell me.
Mary: Well, I don't trust you. I think you might make fun of me.
John: You never used to give me the chance to talk to you. Your anger always got in the way.
Mary: I think I have a right to be angry.
John: Maybe you do, but it will always get in the way of our talking to each other if you can't tell me about it. I'm willing to listen.
Mary: Are you?
John: Yes, try me.

This script could go on, reaching deeper and deeper levels. It could also be done over and over until Mary resolves her hesitation about discussing her anger with John.

The journal is an ideal place for this type of conflict to be resolved. Dialoguing like this will, in many instances, bring about catharsis and release old negative emotions and negative programming.

To summarize: The journal should contain one section for each important person in your life, so that you can gain insight and resolution in either positive or negative relationships. The journal process is not just confined to dialoguing with people who are alive; it is often valuable to dialogue with significant others who have died.

The Physical Body

Alcoholics, other addicts, and adult children (those who are raised in alcoholic and other kinds of dysfunctional families), have generally lost contact with their physical selves. Alcoholics and other addicts lose touch with their bodies by drinking and taking drugs; the adult child loses touch due to the trauma of living in an unsafe family. They have lost the ability to listen to what their bodies have to say to them. And yet each one of us has a wealth of wisdom contained in our physical body. We have huge amounts of information stored within us; all we need to do to gain access to this information is to ask.

The physical body section of the personal journal is the section where you can re-establish this relationship with your physical self. In this section, you will begin to communicate with your physical body. This is done by dialoguing with the body.

To dialogue with the body, the same method is used as in the previous example, where Mary dialogued with her ex-husband, John. The steps are:

1. Write a focusing statement about your relationship with your body.

11

2. List the events that have helped shape your body's life.
3. Dialogue with your body.

The following is an example of a dialogue that Eddie had with his body.

Focusing Statement

12/3/82

I really feel out of touch with you, body. I have always felt that you were just something to endure. For many years I hated you and harmed you. Now I am trying to get to know you better and find out what your needs are.

Major Life Milestones

0 to 10 years old
   Having tonsils out
   Getting spanked
   Not liking being tall and thin
   Playing with my penis

10 to 20 years old
   Masturbating
   Not liking being tall
   Not liking sports and getting hurt playing baseball
   Sex with a woman
   Drinking alcohol

20 to 30 years old
   Being hurt in an accident
   Being sick and having an operation
   Taking drugs
   Getting married

30 to 40 years old
Sick all the time from drugs and alcohol
Trying to kill myself
Stopping drinking and doing drugs
Stopping smoking
Starting to exercise, run and swim
Learning about my body

Dialoguing

Eddie: Hello, Body, are you there?
Body: Yes, I am.
Eddie: How are you doing?
Body: O.K.
Eddie: Are you still mad at me?
Body: Well, maybe a little bit. I don't think that you're taking as good care of me as you did a year ago.
Eddie: That's true, I guess.
Body: For sure. You have abused me almost all of our life. What you did to me with alcohol and drugs was terrible. The car wrecks, throwing up, all of that. Even shooting heroin. I never thought that you would do that.
Eddie: Now hold on. That's all in the past. I haven't used alcohol or drugs in four years.
Body: So you think that all you need to do is to stop drinking and all is fine.
Eddie: Yes, I do.
Body: Well, in case you didn't notice it, I still need care. How about some exercise and vitamins. How about eating right. Some of this garbage you feed me sucks.
Eddie: I know that I've fallen down, but I will try to get back on an exercise program and eat better. I

know that I can, all I need to do is to just do it.
Will you help me out?

Body: *Sure, remember I have your own best interests*
at heart. Just take care of me and I'll be
around for a long time.

Eddie: *O.K. I will try, and I will stay more in touch with*
you.

Dialoguing, as we can see in the above example, can bring surprising results. Most alcoholics like Eddie, have spent a lot of time and energy doing very unhealthy, hostile and almost lethal things to their bodies. It is vital to come to terms with and to be at peace with the physical self. When this occurs, the body itself, through dialoguing, can use its wisdom to inform us about what we need to stay healthy.

Dreams

How often have you wakened in the morning with the memory of a dream? The memory of the dream is clear, and as you lie in bed you realize that an important piece of the puzzle of your life has fallen into place. You have had a profound insight about yourself. You remind yourself that you must remember this important piece of information. After you have been awake for an hour or so, the memory of the dream begins to fade. You still have a sense that something important has happened, but by this time you are unsure as to what took place in your dream. When lunchtime rolls around, you have forgotten the dream altogether.

The above experience has happened to most of us. It is fortunate, I suppose, that we do not recall most of our dreams. If we did our minds would certainly be cluttered with vast amounts of information. Very special experiences happen when we dream; our dreams represent a part of our living process that we don't really understand. It has been established, however, that dreams play an important part in our day-to-day mental health. People who have been deprived of dreaming often show a marked deterioration in their mental health. It has been my experience, both privately and as a counselor that dreams play an important part in the recovery process. During the dream state, we sometimes process and resolve the trauma of the past and heal the wounds of being raised in a dysfunctional family.

If you have, and use, a section in your journal to record the dreams that you feel are important, then the dreams will not fade away. When your dreams are written and recorded, they become concrete, and you will remember them. Not only will you remember the dream, but often you will retain the sense of completion and resolution that sometimes happens during dreaming.

Bob, a former client of mine who was both a recovering alcoholic and recovering child of an alcoholic family, is a clear example of the resolution process that sometimes happens during dreams. Bob's father was an alcoholic who died of alcoholism before Bob entered his own recovery. During group therapy sessions Bob expressed the deep anger that he felt toward his father. He felt that his anger toward his father was so deep and so intense that it would never go away.

Bob came to group for over a year. During one group session he reported to the group that he had had a dream about his father and that although he still felt some anger toward him, most of the anger seemed to have been lifted from him during the dream. He had recorded the dream in his journal and brought it in to share with the group. Below is a portion of Bob's dream.

8/13/84

The dream had Dad and me in it. We were camping out in the mountains. Mom and Dave (little brother) were there too. Dad and me got into an argument and started to fight. We fought up and down the mountain., I was angry and afraid at the same time. We fought for a long time, until I was too tired to fight anymore. Then I left. When I came back I was an adult, and he was still there. I knew that if we fought, I would win and hurt him. So did he. We just sat down and had breakfast. I felt no anger or fear. I felt light and at ease. Then I woke up. I was amazed, I still felt no fear or anger.

Bob credits the clearness of his memory of the dream to recording the dream in his journal as soon as he woke up. He felt that the dream was a turning point in his recovery process, and that if he had not recorded it, he would have stayed longer in his anger at his father. Several years after Bob left group, I asked him about the dream. He said that the old anger had not returned, and that occasionally he re-reads the journal entry about that dream.

Bob's experience is not an isolated incident. Many people have had experiences like Bob's. Dreaming is a mysterious element in the recovery process. Through dreaming we often resolve and put to rest the emotions of anger, fear and hurt. Recording dreams in the journal helps you remember and to make the resolution process real and concrete.

Meditation

Having a meditation section can be helpful in several ways. Here you can record what type of meditation you are doing, how you feel about the meditation, whether anything important happens during the meditation. It is valuable to have a record of these feelings and experiences.

Synthesis

The synthesis section is the place in the journal that provides space for the writer to tie up the loose ends of his life. Here he can record his insights and discoveries, the coming together of his ideas and intuitions. This can be the place for him to chronicle the spiritual awarenesses and experiences that he has had on his life journey. I have intentionally left out examples and detailed instructions for this section. My purpose was to allow the reader to be free from preconceived ideas of how to do this section, and to let the creative intuitive process guide the work.

I feel that the sections outlined above are important to the beginning journal writer. But this is just a start. The personal journal is not limited to the sections we have discussed. You may add as many sections to the journal as you wish. There is no limit to the size of the personal journal. Its size is governed by need and is limited only by the creativity of the writer. The journal will unfold and grow as you grow. Experiment with your journal. It is important to stress that the journal need not be limited to just the written word. Many times our unconscious gives us messages in symbols or creative impulses. There could be a section for symbols and their interpretations, and a section for drawings, poetry and other artwork as well.

Let the personal journal unfold and develop at its own rate. The journal will be unique and it will take on a character of its own. It will speak to you.

This is your journal. You need not show any part of this journal to anyone, even your counselor. This is your private document, although you can share its content if you choose.

I have found that when a person in therapy keeps a personal journal, the counseling session can become a richer and deeper experience. Those in therapy are usually more than willing to share what they have written. Keeping a journal helps them feel that they are taking an active part in their own growth.

The journal is like a tapestry. When we weave the words of our lives in the journal, we create a beautiful work of art. Against the background of this artwork we dance and weave, discover and grow. Journal-keeping is an art. Like any art, it must be practiced. The journal is also like a musical instrument and should be played. At some point in the process of journal-writing, the journal writes itself, just as a musical instrument seems to play itself after the musician has become one with it.

The journal is a tool that can be used when necessary. The process of journal-writing is a skill that you can use for the rest of your life.

This is a gift.

Dr. Ira Progoff has developed a journal called the Intensive Journal and has established a series of workshops that teach how to set up and use an Intensive Journal. He also has written *"At A Journal Workshop"* and *"The Practice of Process Meditation"*. These books are musts for the serious student of the journal. I encourage you to read them and if possible, attend one of the Intensive Journal Workshops.

2

Meditation

 People have been using meditative techniques for thousands of years, and today millions of people meditate on a regular basis. In this section, we will explore some different ways of meditating and why meditating can be useful to the recovering person (whether recovering from an addiction or a dysfunctional family).

Most people seem to have a lot of trouble turning off the constant internal dialogue that goes on inside their heads. In order to find serenity and emotional stability, it is necessary to stop, or slow down, this internal dialogue. Meditation is a very effective way to halt or slow down this constant flow of thoughts.

The effects of meditation are four-fold. First, it assists the physical body with deep relaxation and the letting go of the physical manifestations of stress, Second, meditation helps to calm the emotional aspects of a person's nature. Third, meditation helps to give the meditator a clearer mental frame and the ability to focus more keenly. Fourth, meditation opens up a channel to the meditator's higher levels of consciousness and spiritual awareness.

These may seem to be rather extravagant claims, but they are not. One of the greatest gifts that you can give to yourself is the gift of meditation.

Simply put, meditation is a process by which a person intentionally quiets his mind so he can become aware of his inner nature, his true self.

There are many ways to meditate. I am going to introduce you to two basic meditative methods, Breathing Meditation and Mantra Meditation.

Breathing Meditation

When we practice breathing meditation, all we do is become aware of the process of our breathing.

Sit in a straight-backed chair, or in a cross-legged position on the floor. It is important that the person who is meditating be comfortable; it is hard to concentrate on breathing when you are in pain. It is, however, important to keep your back as straight as possible, while remaining relaxed. Close your eyes and pay attention to your breath as it flows in and out of your body. You do not have to control your breath, but breathe in a natural way.

Pay attention to the air as it enters your nose; feel how cool it is. Feel how warm your outgoing breath is. Focus attention on your breathing in a relaxed, noncontrolling manner. Be aware of the process of your breath as it flows in and out of your body. If thoughts come into your mind, relax and let them go.

Do this for about five to ten minutes. This is meditating on the breath. Easy, isn't it?

Mantra Meditation

When you meditate on a sound, you are using a technique called Mantra Meditation. In this type of meditation, instead of focusing the attention on breathing, you focus on a sound.

Many people have difficulty concentrating on breathing. They find it much easier to focus on a sound and repeat that sound over and over. As in breathing meditation, sit either cross-legged on the floor or in a straight-backed chair. Either position is O.K. The important thing is to be comfortable and to sit upright.

When using mantra meditation, it is important to pick a sound that has very little or no conscious meaning. A sound that is used many times in this type of meditation is the word "one", which is repeated over and over. The sound that I like is "So-Hum". It has a pleasant rhythm. The sound of "OM" is also very widely used for mantra meditation. Any of the above sounds are fine to use.

Sit and say the sound softly, over and over, saying it softer and softer each time until you are no longer saying the sound out loud, but are repeating it silently inside of your head. Do this for five to ten minutes. When thoughts come, all you need do is gently return to the sound. Find a quiet place to sit, focus on the sound and say it silently over and over.

It is natural to forget that you are meditating and to start to think about other things. When this occurs, just refocus on the breath or the sound and gently return to meditating.

Many people get frustrated and angry because they cannot concentrate and their minds wander. This is very natural and happens to almost everyone. The meditative process will be effective even if most of the time meditating is spent in wandering thoughts. For the beginning meditator, the most important aspects of meditation are the willingness to sit and meditate, and to continue to return to the meditative state when the thoughts wander.

Meditate the first thing in the morning, before you drink coffee or smoke. I believe that this helps to start the day with an attitude of serenity. Meditating in the morning, before coffee or cigarettes, also interrupts the addictive cycle of these two drugs. This enhances the possibility of letting go of these addictions.

If, however, it is difficult to meditate in the morning, select a more convenient time. Although I prefer the morning, anytime during the day will do.

It is very important to agree upon a length of time that you will meditate. The generally accepted length of time for meditation is twenty minutes once or twice a day. My experience has been that many newly-recovering people have a great deal of difficulty sitting still for that length of time, so it should be considered not as an absolute, but as something to aim for.

On the other hand, some people will wish to sit in meditation for hours at a time. This extreme should also be avoided. Many recovering persons have a tendency to overdo things. Then they get burned out on them.

Start off meditating for five to ten minutes once a day. If you do this on a regular basis, then you will naturally increase the length of time that you meditate. You will grow in meditation at your own rate.

When a person begins to meditate and quiets the internal dialogue, many things happen. When the mind becomes quiet, the meditator makes room for many repressed emotions and experiences to bubble to the surface. When these repressed feelings surface, then the meditator can let go of them.

Picture the mind as a lake, whose surface is full of ripples caused by the wind of our thoughts. When we meditate, that wind is slowed down and stopped. When this happens, we are allowed a glimpse into the depths of our very being. When we look into these depths, we are free to let go of many old painful emotions and thoughts.

This is truly a gift.

3

Affirmations

We are what we think. There is a great deal of power in the thoughts, spoken words and written statements that we make about ourselves. A direct correlation exists between the way a person thinks about himself and how he behaves. It is difficult for many of us to imagine how much of our own reality we create by how we think and speak.

Current research does, however, indicate that to a large extent, we create our own realities with our thoughts. Research in the health sciences definitely proves that thoughts and attitudes contribute to the healing process, and that these same thoughts and attitudes also contribute to ill health. The difference is whether these thoughts are positive or negative.

Alcoholism is a disease of the body, emotions, mind and spirit. There are very few other diseases that succeed in isolating a person from loved ones, and from the human community, like alcoholism does. As a person becomes more and more a slave to alcoholism, he becomes more and more withdrawn, and the way he thinks about himself becomes increasingly negative. These negative thoughts are also reinforced by the way the alcoholic's family and the rest of the world treat him.

An alcoholic does not know who he is. His self-image is very poor, his thoughts about others are negative, and the way he speaks about himself is negative.

In recovery, after the alcoholic is not drinking, these negative thoughts and feelings continue to plague him and can continue to do so for a long time. There are many recovered alcoholics who have stopped drinking, but still have the same old negative thinking and feeling patterns. A vital part of the recovery process is the reconstruction and integration of the positive thoughts and the rebuilding of positive self-image.

A powerful tool for the rebuilding of a positive image is the creative use of affirmations.

Affirmations are positive thoughts that a person deliberately introduces into his or her consciousness, so that the old, negative programming is replaced by new and positive thoughts.

The alcoholic's negative programming runs deep and comes from two basic sources. The first is compulsive drinking itself. The irrational and insane behavior caused by compulsive drinking produces feelings of shame and guilt in the alcoholic. These feelings of shame and guilt are not experienced directly but are often translated into negative feelings of self-worth and self-image that the alcoholic keeps in his unconscious mind.

Second, negative programming also comes from the way the alcoholic learned to view himself when he was a child. As a child, the alcoholic or the child of an alcoholic, like all children, received both verbal and nonverbal messages from the important adults in his life. Many times these messages were translated into negative programming. This is also true for those people who were raised in alcoholic families and who did not become active (drinking) alcoholics. As adults this negative programming is still carried around in the unconscious mind.

A person who is in the process of recovery from alcoholism or being raised in a dysfunctional family and who has this negative programming is constantly in a state of internal conflict. He feels good about himself for being in recovery, but he still has this old unconscious programming telling him that he is a "bad person".

Over a period of time affirmations can replace those old negative programs. It is vital to remember that affirmations are not used to repress feelings. They are not used to stuff emotions. Alcoholics and adult children have a great deal of experience with stuffing feelings and emotions; we don't need another technique. The process of releasing stuffed negative emotions must occur for the alcoholic or adult child to grow. Affirmations create a new and fresh point of view, rather than just replace the old ideas.

There are a number of different ways to do affirmations. The ways that I have found to be the most effective are:

1. Spoken silently to oneself
2. Said out loud
3. Spoken out loud to another person
4. Spoken into a recorder and played back
5. Written down on paper

The following statements are guidelines that are helpful when using affirmations:

1. Affirmations are positive statements. We teach people to affirm the positive, rather than reinforce the negative.
2. Affirmations are most effective when they are short and to the point. Keep them simple.
3. Affirmations are kept in the present.
4. Affirmations affirm what one desires, rather than what one wants to get rid of.
5. Affirmations take time to get results. They should not be put on a timetable; the results will unfold at their own speed.
6. Affirmations are repeated each day. It is the repetition of the positive affirmation that produces the desired result.

Some time ago I had a client named Helen. Helen was married to an alcoholic. Her husband had been sober for four years but had returned to drinking, and had been drinking for about two years when Helen came to me for counseling.

Like many people who are married to alcoholics, Helen was raised in an alcoholic family and had an extremely low self-image. She could not imagine what she could do to change her current living situation, but she knew that she had to do something because she was in a lot of emotional pain. Like many women in her situation, she also blamed herself for her husband's drinking problems.

After Helen and I had been in two counseling sessions, we worked out a simple affirmation that she could do at home and at work. The affirmation was, "I, Helen, love myself."

Helen's instructions were to say this affirmation ten times to herself every morning.

"I, Helen, love myself."
"I, Helen, love myself."
"I, Helen, love myself."
"I, Helen, love myself."
"I, Helen, love myself."
"I, Helen, love myself."
"I, Helen, love myself."
"I, Helen, love myself."
"I, Helen, love myself."
"I, Helen, love myself."

Helen's self-image was so poor that at first she was unable to say the affimation out loud. After a number of weeks she could say the affirmation out loud to herself, at which point I had her say the affirmation out loud to herself each morning while looking in her bedroom mirror.

It was a major turning point in Helen's life when, during a counseling session, she was able to look me in the eyes and tell me, *"I, Helen, love myself."*

Each person is different, and affirmations should be tailored to the individual needs. In Helen's case she needed to start very gently, with her saying the affirmation first silently to herself, then out loud to the mirror and finally out loud to me.

Over the months that Helen and I were in the counseling relationship, she continued to do her affirmation and her feelings of self-love got stronger and stronger. The result of this work was that Helen finally left the unhealthy relationship and rebuilt her life. I received a telephone call from her a year after she moved out of town and she was doing fine. And still doing her affirmation.

I have received some very positive feedback from clients who have used their affirmations in creative ways. A powerful method for using affirmations is to have the person record the affirmation onto a tape and play the tape back at convenient times such as on the car stereo while driving to and from work, or playing the tape when doing housework. As the tape is being played back, the person can either just listen to the tape, or say the affirmation along with the recording.

The most powerful way to use affirmations is to write them down on paper. This method strongly reinforces the affirmation because as the affirmation is being written it is seen, said to one's self and "felt" as the act of writing is taking place.

Do not overload yourself with affirmations. Having four or five affirmations to work with can be very time-consuming and discouraging. One or two affirmations at a time is best. Remember: You are learning not only how to use affirmations, but also how to create them.

Changes in attitude and point of view occur very rapidly with people who use written affirmations. Written affirmations are most effective when written ten to twenty times each day. I am partial to morning, but any time during the day is effective. (I choose morning because if I don't do things in the morning, I have a tendency not to ever get around to them.)

To be most powerful, the written affirmation is done in the first person (I), the second person (you), and the third person (he or she). Here is an example involving a former client of mine named Steven.

Like many other chemically-dependent people, Steven was having a difficult time getting in touch with his emotions. He felt very "stuck". He knew that he was blocking emotions, but he did not know how to get "unstuck".

The affirmation that we worked out for Steven was:

"I, Steven, am capable and willing to experience all of my emotions."

This part of the affirmation is written in the first person and makes the statement that even with old negative ideas about being unable to express emotions, he, Steven, is affirming that today he can express emotions. (Remember that to be effective, affirmations are done in the present tense.)

"You, Steven, are capable and willing to experience all of your emotions."

This part of the affirmation is written in the second person and makes the statement that although Steven was once taught that showing emotions was unacceptable behavior, today he is allowed to show emotion.

"He, Steven, is capable and willing to experience all of his emotions."

This part of the affirmation is written in the third person and makes the statement that regardless of the role models that Steven had, and regardless of what people said about him, Steven is capable and willing to express his emotions today.

The whole affirmation was:

"I, Steven, am capable and willing to experience all of my emotions."

"You, Steven, are capable and willing to experience all of your emotions."

"He, Steven, is capable and willing to experience all of his emotions."

An important point to remember is that when strong positive affirmations are used, they will, in most cases, bring up strong negative feelings from the person's subconscious. When a person who has had strong negative programming uses a positive affirmation, the negative feelings that are a part of that old programming will surface. This is particularly true when the affirmation is being written.

When you are writing an affirmation, it is important to acknowledge these negative feelings. This acknowledgment is a part of the process of letting go of the old programming. During the process of writing the affirmation, you must also write down the negative feelings you experience. I have found that jotting down the negative thoughts after writing the affirmation is the most effective method for noting the negative response.

After you have written the affirmations, you can review the negative responses. These will give insights into the unconscious negative programming that is standing in the way of the fulfillment of your affirmation. After you have written the negative responses for approximately four days, you will have a good idea of what is standing in the way of the affirmation. At this point you discontinue writing the negative responses and just write the affirmation.

The negative responses that surface during writing the affirmations make excellent material for discussion during possible counseling sessions, or for writing about in the personal journal (See Chapter 1).

Many times, as you write your affirmation, you will move from negative responses to more positive responses. During this process of moving from the negative to the positive, you may even find yourself writing encouraging statements about the affirmation.

Continuing to use Steven as an example, the affirmation and his responses were as follows:

"I, Steven, am capable and willing to experience all of my emotions." (No, I can't do that.)

"You, Steven, are capable and willing to experience all of your emotions." (I was told that it was bad to show emotions.)

"He, Steven, is capable and willing to experience all of his emotions." (No, I'm not.)

"I, Steven, am capable and willing to experience all of my emotions." (What if someone sees me cry?)

"You, Steven, are capable and willing to experience all of your emotions." (I'm afraid to let people in.)

"He, Steven, is capable and willing to express all of his emotions." (I feel so sad.)

"I, Steven, am capable and willing to experience all of my emotions." (Dad never cried.)

"You, Steven, are capable and willing to experience all of your emotions." (This makes me feel sick.)

33

"He, Steven, is capable and willing to express all of his emotions." (I won't be a man if I feel.)

"I, Steven, am capable and willing to experience all of my emotions." (I'm afraid of what's bottled up inside me.)

"You, Steven, are capable and willing to experience all of your emotions." (I'll lose control.)

"He, Steven, is capable and willing to express all of his emotions." (The last time I cried I was ten.)

"I, Steven, am capable and willing to experience all of my emotions." (Maybe I can.)

"You, Steven, are capable and willing to experience all of your emotions." (It might not be so bad.)

"He, Steven, is capable and willing to express all of his emotions." (I think I will be able to.)

As can be seen in the above example, while Steven was writing his affirmation, he moved from the negative responses that he wrote in the beginning, to more positive and encouraging responses.

Change can happen quickly when affirmations are used. Not only can affirmations be used to root out the old negative programming that alcoholics have, but they can also be used to deal with immediate situations that cause fearful responses.

One client called me on the phone and told me that she wanted to call a man that she was interested in to ask him to a party, but she was afraid to make the call. She had to make the call that night because the party was the next day. I asked her what kind of affirmation would fit this situation, and she created this affirmation:

"I, Kim, can ask Joe for a date."

She wrote this several times and then made the telephone call.

Many recovering people have difficulties in relationships. The isolation that is brought about by drinking or coming from a dysfunctional family does not lend itself either to attracting a healthy mate, or to being a healthy partner in a relationship. Some excellent affirmations to use in relationships are:

"I, _____, am a healthy person, and I am capable of having a loving, intimate relationship."

"I, _____, no longer need _____ to make me feel good about myself."

"I love myself and I deserve a good relationship."

Affirmations are not really very new. People have been using them for years, even in the addictions field. How many times have you heard, *"I, _____, am clean and sober today."*? Now that's a powerful affirmation.

Most of us really enjoy doing affirmations. It gives an extremely positive payoff for doing a small amount of work, and helps us feel good about ourselves. Affirmations give an opportunity to take a visible, active part in our growth.

The following is a list of some of the affirmations that I use with my clients on a regular basis:

"Every day in every way I am getting better, better and better."

"I accept all of my feelings as a part of myself."

"The more I love myself, the more I am capable of loving."

"I am a whole, healthy human being."

"My life is unfolding as it should."

"I, _____, am lovable."

"I, _____, am loving."

"I, _____, deserve love."

"My true self is my sober self."

"My life has meaning and purpose."

"I am living my life one day at a time."

"Today I can stay sober and happy."

Many of my clients have a spiritual unrest within them, and almost to a person, they have a desire to grow in a spiritual direction. I encourage them in their personal spiritual quests, for I have found that it is this inward searching and the spiritual way of life that give the lives of many recovered people a sense of meaning and purpose.

Affirmations used in a spiritual context are powerful. I have found that people who seek to expand and grow spiritually use this type of affirmation with great enthusiasm and effectiveness. Below are some examples of affirmations that have a spiritual dimension and direction.

"My higher self is guiding me in everything I do."

"The Light within me is creating miracles in my life today."

"I am letting go and letting God."

"I, _____, am living in the presence of divine love and light."

"I, _____, am at one with the spirit of the universe."

If you are using a personal journal, it is useful to create a section for written affirmations. You will then be able to track your use of affirmations over a period of time. This will demonstrate, first-hand, what a powerful tool affirmations are.

You have the wisdom to know which affirmations will work for you. After you have been using affirmations for a while, you will, in many cases, change the affirmations that you were originally using. This is a wonderful step. Re-create your affirmations. Affirmations are a gift that you will be able to use for the rest of your life.

4

Creative
Visualization

 It is the nature of the human being to think and to imagine. We are what we think and are capable of becoming what we imagine. There is a power in our imagination that is, as yet, not completely understood. We do know that the ability to use creative imagination is open to everyone. All humans have the ability to imagine and to dream.

The process of creative visualization is the conscious directing of the imagination to produce a desired result. The human mind is a powerful resource, and its ability and potential are to a large extent unknown. We do know, however, that using the imagination in a controlled and directed manner can produce results in healing the physical body, stabilizing the emotions, quieting the mind and communicating with the inner spirit.

Each one of us has the ability to use inner vision. This inner vision is, however, not the same for each individual. Most of the people that I have worked with have had the ability to "see pictures" in their mind's eye. There is, however, a sizable number who dislike visualization because they cannot "see" these pictures. These people "see" in a different way; their inner experience is more a feeling rather than a seeing. Others "think about" what they want to visualize; they don't see pictures or feel. Some do all of the above, or at any given time, do one or the other.

The important point is, we as human beings have the ability to have inner visions, and have the capacity to imagine. People do this in different ways; the results are the same.

Creative visualization is a powerful tool that you can use. It is important to remember that what we dream to be, we can become, and that we imagine can come to pass.

Thoughts are energy. They have power. When the powerful energy of thoughts is directed and focused, the results can be amazing. Most people take their thoughts for granted. They believe that since they have a seemingly endless and constant stream of thoughts flowing through their minds, these thoughts are unimportant and carry no power. But thoughts are powerful, even random or trivial ones, and they always transmit a powerful message to our subconscious.

The recovering alcoholic has been caught up in negative thoughts and behaviors. Long after the drinking has stopped, these negative patterns can cause emotional pain and physical ill health. Through the use of creative visualization, the recovering person can move away from his old, negative thinking patterns.

The above is also true for ACoAs. Children who grow up in the alcoholic family system have developed negative thought and behavior patterns in order to survive. For adults, these patterns cause pain and confusion. Creative visualization can change these negative thought patterns to positive ones.

Thoughts and imagination have energy and power. When we direct our thoughts and imagination in a positive direction, a positive result is produced. Conversely, if thoughts and imagination are directed in a negative direction, then we can expect negative outcomes. Fear attracts more fear and anger produces nothing but anger.

The following story is an example of negative imagination in action.

A man was driving along a deserted country road. It was late in the evening and very dark. Suddenly there was a loud sound, like a gunshot; the man pulled to the side of the road, got out of the car, and discovered that he had a flat tire. When he opened his trunk, he found that he had left his tire jack at home.

Off in the distance the man could see a light in a farmhouse window. Not wanting to spend the night in the car, he decided that he would walk to the farm and ask the farmer if he would lend him a tire jack.

As he started to walk along the road to the farmhouse, the man began to imagine what would happen when he talked to the farmer. His thoughts went something like this:

"It's late and the farmer is most likely asleep. When I ring his doorbell, I'll wake him up and he'll probably be angry."

"Farmers don't generally like city people like me anyway."

"He will probably tell me to get off of his property."

"He might even have a gun and run me off, or turn his dogs loose on me."

"Farmers are all a bunch of ill-tempered jerks anyway."

"They love to give strangers like me a hard time."

By the time the man reached the farmhouse, he had become angry and defensive. When he rang the doorbell and the farmer opened the door, the man shouted angrily at the farmer, "You can stick your jack where the sun doesn't shine, I wouldn't take it if you offered it to me!" The man then turned and stalked away from the amazed and confused farmer.

This may seem like a far-fetched story, but time and again I have seen my clients imagine themselves into situations that are not any less absurd than the above.

On the other hand, I have also seen clients let go of old negative thoughts through the use of creative visualization. The mind can be trained, and it can be controlled. Thoughts can be redirected, and the negative imaginings that have become part of a person's thoughts can become positive visualizations. The process is simple.

The basic steps to the process of creative visualization are:

1. Have a clear and specific idea or picture of the desired objective or goal.
2. Set the desired objective or goal in the mind.
3. Focus on the objective or goal often.
4. Give positive energy (good thoughts) to the goal or objective.

If you have had years of practice using visualization and imagination in negative ways, it is important that you proceed slowly and simply. Doing easy and simple visualizations will quickly produce a history of successes, and will give you the confidence that creative visualization will work for you.

The first step is to realize that you can use your imagination in a healthy and constructive way.

A former client of mine, Ken, was fearful of using his imagination. For years, he had always thought in negative terms, and when any situation came up, all he could see was a negative outcome. Thus, most of his important life situations resulted in negative outcomes. Ken did not want to use his mind and inner vision, he did not trust them.

In order for Ken to gain the experience of having positive results using his imagination, I took him step-by-step through a relaxation exercise using creative visualization. I have found that this step-by-step procedure works extremely well with people like Ken who have had a lot of negative experiences from their imaginations.

To begin this creative visualization relaxation exercise, I had Ken lie down, become quiet, close his eys and listen to the sound of my voice.

(. . . indicates a pause of approximately 10 to 15 seconds)

Relax . . . Breathe normally and without straining or trying to control . . . Continue to concentrate on your breath . . . Allow yourself to breathe easily and slowly . . .

(Allow one to two minutes to be still and concentrate on breathing) . . .

Continue to breathe, slowly and quietly . . . Allow your mind to scan your body . . . Find any areas in your body where you experience tension or strain. When you find an area that is tense, direct your thoughts to that area of your body, and with every out breath imagine that you are releasing and letting go of the tension and strain . . .

(Allow one to two minutes to experience letting go of the tension, occasionally remembering to breathe and to relax) . . .

Relax and continue to breathe . . . Now I want you to imagine that you are in a place where you can be totally relaxed, a place where you can be completely comfortable and at ease, without disturbances or interruptions . . . This place of deep relaxation could be a sunlit meadow, or a hot bath. It can be any place that you choose to be . . .

(Allow a minute or two to find a place of relaxation) . . .

Nod your head when you have this place of deep relaxation . . . Continue to stay in your place of deep relaxation . . .

If other thoughts interrupt you, or your mind wanders to another subject, gently remind yourself to return to your place of relaxation . . .

You are now getting ready to become more and more aware of the outside world . . . Remember that you can return to this place of deep relaxation anytime that you wish, just by breathing slowly and remembering your special place of relaxation . . . Become aware of your body . . . Feel the weight of your clothes against your skin . . . Become aware of your breath . . . When you are ready, open your eyes.

Ken had a place of relaxation that was on the shore of a quiet blue lake. He pictured himself sitting on the shore of this lake during a summer afternoon, with the warm summer sun shining down on him. Ken found that when he began to tense up, or when he wanted to relax at night after work, all he had to do was to imagine himself back at his quiet blue lake. Then he became more relaxed.

You can do the above visualization by taping it and playing it back, or by having another person read it to you.

After you have done this relaxation visualization several times, you will begin to notice that, by using the power of imagination, you will be able to relax when you are feeling tense and uptight. This is an important step. Once you have a record of success with using creative visualizations, you can move on to more complex visualizations.

Releasing Anger

All of the clients that I have worked with have suffered, at one level or another, from anger and resentment. Using creative visualization to assist a client to release this anger and resentment is extremely effective. Many people simply don't know how to begin to let go of it.

Accepting that the anger is there is the first step in the process of letting go of it. Unfortunately, many people get stuck in the acceptance step and keep experiencing their anger, rage and resentment over and over. They have done all that they know to do to let go of these feelings. They have talked about it, written about it, found out where it comes from, talked (if possible) to the other person about their anger, and still they have not been able to release it.

Kay, a former client of mine, is an excellent example of how to use creative visualization to let go of anger. Kay had been involved in a relationship, and when it ended, she still felt a lot of anger and resentment toward her ex-boyfriend. Kay had done all that she knew to let go of her anger; she had written about it, discussed it, even confronted her ex-boyfriend with it. Although Kay felt that these actions had produced relief, she still felt that she was holding onto anger. She really wanted to let go, but she did not know how.

After Kay and I had discussed her anger, we decided that doing a creative visualization might help her to let go of it.

I asked Kay to find a comfortable position, to close her eyes and listen to the sound of my voice. I told her that she was in control and could open her eyes any time she wished. Then I guided Kay through the following creative visualization:

(. . . indicates a pause of 10 to 15 seconds)

Relax and listen to the sound of your breath

. . . Pay attention to how it feels to breathe . . . Relax and go inward . . . Continue to breathe; with every outgoing breath, feel yourself becoming more and more relaxed . . . Scan your body; if you find any areas of tension or discomfort, with every outgoing breath let go of the tension . . . Nod your head to let me know when you are totally relaxed and at ease . . .

(Here I waited for Kay to nod; the process took approximately three minutes) . . .

Picture the man that you have the resentment against . . . Picture him in great detail; see the color of his hair, notice what color his eyes are, be aware of what he is wearing . . . When you have a clear picture of this man, let me know by nodding your head . . .

(Kay nods her head) . . .

Now I want you to surround this man with a golden light . . . Hold him in this light . . . Think thoughts of forgiveness and love towards this man . . . Keeping him in the golden light, say to him "I, Kay, forgive you" . . . Say this several times to yourself . . . Now become aware of the outer world . . . Pay attention to your breathing . . . When you feel ready, open your eyes.

I asked Kay to do this visualization once in the morning and once in the evening. At first she felt little relief from her resentment and anger, but after a week of doing this visualization, she began to have kinder feelings towards this man, and after just a few weeks she had no resentment.

This technique does work, and it works fast. I have

had clients get rid of their anger and resentments after only a few sessions of using creative visualization. Sometimes, when the anger is extremely deep-seated, the process may take more time. But if you are willing to do the visualization, the anger and resentment will leave.

Once again it is important to remember that the creative visualization process is not used to repress emotions. If you are not ready or willing to let go of the anger (or any other negative emotion), you will experience that emotion more intensely when you attempt to use creative visualization. This is an ideal time to process this emotion.

Getting in Touch with Your Higher Self

Creative visualization can be used to achieve many different goals. It is particularly effective when used by recovering people to get in contact with their higher natures or higher selves.

The higher self is that part of the human conscious-ness which represents the highest aspirations of the human spirit. It is that aspect of human nature from which love, beauty, unity and the desire to grow toward a higher ideal radiate. It is from the higher self that inspiration and intuitive awareness spring. The higher self is the well of the soul. It has a connection to universal truth and wisdom that defies logic.

The higher self can be effectively contacted by using creative visualization. I have never had a client who did not wish to find out more about his or her spiritual nature. It is through contact and dialogue with the higher self that the recovering person can achieve and maintain a rapport with his spiritual self. In many instances, it is this relationship that gives the person a sense of purpose that he has been yearning for to feel complete.

The visualization that I have found to be most successful in guiding people to the awareness of their higher selves follows.

(. . . Indicates a pause of 10 to 15 seconds)

Find a comfortable position, either sitting or lying down on your back. Relax . . . Pay attention to your breathing . . . Feel your breath going in and out of your nose . . . Feel the coolness of the air as it enters your nose . . . Relax . . . Continue to breathe in an uncontrolled and relaxed manner . . . Allow your breath to come freely . . .

(Pause and allow 2 to 3 minutes to pass) . . .

When you are relaxed, scan your body for any points or areas of tension of pain . . . If you find an area of stress, breathe into it and allow the tension and the pain to flow away with your outgoing breath . . .

Imagine yourself standing on a path in a large forest . . . It is a woods full of large trees . . . The trees are full of leaves . . . The sunlight filters down through the trees and gives the forest a twilight feeling . . . You begin to walk along the path . . . As you walk along this path, you see how beautiful the forest is . . . Ahead of you there is a clearing . . . a clearing at the end of the path . . . As you walk toward the clearing, you realize that it is a meadow . . . You step out of the forest into the meadow . . . It is very pretty . . . There are flowers and butterflies... You slowly follow the path across the meadow ... At the end of the path on the other side of the meadow is a tall mountain ...

As you walk toward the mountain, you see that there is a white stone stairway that leads up the side of the mountain ... You cannot see the top of the mountain, but you begin to climb the stairs ...

As you climb, you realize that you are feeling lighter and freer, as if you had left all of your cares and troubles below ... You continue to climb and you continue to feel better and better ...

When you reach the top of the white stairway, you see a large, white stone building ... It is very beautiful ... You walk to the steps leading into this building and climb them ... At the top of the steps is a large door ... You open the door and enter the building ... The room that you step into is large and beautifully furnished ... It has rich wall hangings and is filled with the type of furnishings that you like ... You stand in the room for a moment and take in the beauty of it ...

At the far end of the room you see a door ... You slowly walk across the room to the door ... As you approach this door, you feel at peace and relaxed ... You know that on the other side of the door you will meet a being who is full of wisdom and love ... You reach out and open the door and step into a room ... The room is simply furnished ... But it is beautiful ...

As you stand there in this room you became aware of another presence in the room with you ... This presence radiates love and wisdom ... You have no fear or doubts ... You stand there and bask in the love of this being ... If you have any questions that you feel that you need or want to ask this being, ask them now . . .

(Pause for 2 or 3 minutes to ask any questions that you may have) . . .

As you say farewell to this being, you have the knowledge that you may return to this place any time you wish . . .

You leave the small room and enter the large hall . . . You walk slowly through the hall to the door and go out to the steps . . . You go down the steps and walk to the stairway leading down the mountain . . . When you reach the stairway you turn and look back at the large white building . . . You know that you can return there whenever you wish . . .

You turn and go down the stairway . . .

When you reach the bottom of the stairway, you walk along the path, across the meadow . . . You continue across the meadow on the path and enter the forest . . . You feel fine and at peace with yourself . . . As you walk along the path through the forest, you reflect on the events that have just happened . . . You feel fine . . . As you continue to walk along the forest path, you begin to feel that you are back in your body . . . You pay attention to your breath as you breathe in and out . . . When you are ready, open your eyes.

The above visualization generally takes about twenty minutes. It is important that enough time is left at the end of the visualization for you to process your experiences. Most times, after this type of visualization, you will feel a need to share what has occurred. This opening up to the higher self is an important step in your growth process. Treat it with respect.

I have used this visualization with many clients; it is powerful. Many times this experience is the beginning of the person's opening up to his or her own inner wisdom, realizing his or her own spiritual nature. You can use this visualization by recording it on a tape and playing it back, or you could get a friend or counselor to read it to you. Either way the visualization can be very effective.

Creative visualization is a gift that will help you open up to the power of creative imagination. With this gift you can let go of old negative thoughts and refocus your mind on a more positive idea of life and your relation to it. The power of the imagination is unlimited. The mind, when used in a positive way, can open up ways of being that you may never have considered before.

People in recovery need not continue to fear their mind and imagination. They can learn to use them in powerful and creative ways. The imagination can become an ally and a friend.

With creative visualization all things become possible. It can open doorways to the imagination and the creative self. But the possibilites of opening to these aspects of ourselves are dwarfed by the greater potential we have for spiritual growth. Becoming aware of the dimensions of the spirit, and finding a way to get in touch with and have access to, the higher self is possible with the use of creative visualization. This is truly a gift.

5

Positioning

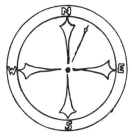

During the ongoing process of our daily lives, we have a periodic need to assess who we are and where we are going. Many of us feel overwhelmed by the day-to-day activities that make up our lives, and it is important to find a way to stop and look at the specific actions that we take, as well as listen to the specific thoughts that we have about ourselves.

Positioning is a way to do this — to stop our individual process and take a look at what we are really doing in our lives. Without positioning we tend to become unaware of the subtle changes of direction that our thinking takes; we could begin to act in a way that is not consistent with the way we *think* we are acting.

Many of the alcoholic clients that I work with are unable to position themselves in the ongoing process of their lives, and it's easy to see why. Through all the years of drinking and drugging, they have been unable to reconcile their behavior with their values. This is part of the disease of addiction. The addict does not act in a manner that is consistent with his value system. So it is no wonder recovered alcoholics have trouble taking stock of themselves. Either they have no previous experience at it, and so do not know where to begin, or else they are horrified by what they find when they take a sober look at the past.

One of the most common complaints that I hear from people in recovery is that they feel overwhelmed by their lives. Things seem out of control. They feel that they are on a roller coaster and that everything in life is just a blur. When I meet with people who feel like this, I try to assist them to find out what is actually happening in their lives, and what their position is in the ongoing process of their lives.

Jan, a former client of mine, first started counseling with the complaint that she felt overwhelmed by life, that things were moving along too fast for her; she never seemed to have time to do the things she enjoyed.

After we had talked for a while, I asked her to tell me three things that she liked to do, that gave her a great deal of pleasure.

Her responses were:

I like to go camping.

I like to go the movies.

I enjoy reading novels.

Jan was very clear on what she liked to do. I asked her to write these things down on a piece of paper. Then I asked her to put the date when she had last done each of these activities. When we compared what she stated she liked to do with the last date she had actually done it, she was amazed.

She had not gone camping for over two years. She was not sure when she had been to the movies last, but it had been more than several months ago. She had been reading the same novel for over six months, never seeming to have time to finish it.

When Jan and I first discussed the things she did for pleasure, she talked about the above activities as if these were things she did on a regular basis, but her thinking and her actions clearly did not match up. In her mind she "thought" she was doing fun things but in reality she wasn't. She had become so caught up in the movement of her life and the fast pace of her day-to-day existence that she had forgotten to have fun.

This is easy to do. Many of my clients forget to have fun; (and so do counselors). We forget to do the things that give us pleasure. We don't realize what we are doing on a daily basis; we draw from the memory of having had pleasure in the past and then wonder why the present seems so unfulfilling.

When beginning a positioning session, I ask a client to write out what he likes, and write out the date when he last did the activity. The writing brings the activity into focus. The client stops the process of his life for a moment and looks directly at what he is doing in light of what he thinks he is doing.

When Jan compared her list and the corresponding dates, she easily realized why she was feeling over-whelmed. She and I made a contract that during the next week she would take time out to do at least one of the things on her fun list. Over a period of time Jan reincorporated the fun activities into her life. The feeling of being swept along by life and of being out of control left her. Her life became much more balanced.

Another important aspect of using the fun list is that in some instances, parts of the list will prove to be invalid. A person may think that he enjoys a particular activity, but when he actually does the activity, he finds that he no longer enjoys doing it.

I asked Joe, a man who came to me because he felt that his life was dull and uninteresting, to make a fun list. His list was:

I like to hunt.

I like to fish.

I like boating.

Joe had become caught up in the same trap as Jan; he had allowed his life to become so busy that he did not do anything for fun. We made a contract that he would begin to reintegrate fun activities into his life. After several experiences with hunting, Joe found out that he really did not enjoy hunting. The only reason he had gone hunting in the past was to get away from his family and drink. With this discovery, Joe was able to let go of the idea that he liked to hunt. He stopped wasting energy thinking about an activity that he did not enjoy. He could then explore new ways to have fun and integrate them into his life.

A majority of people who come from dysfunctional families simply don't know how to have fun. They never learned how. The concept of playing or having fun is, for the most part, missing in an alcoholic household. Children in such an environment rarely learn how to set aside time for fun activities. When they grow up and leave the alcoholic family, they have a good chance of either becoming caught up in their own addiction, or pairing up with someone already addicted. This addictive pattern continues the joyless existence they experienced in childhood, when there was little time or space to do things "just for fun".

When a client has difficulty making up a fun list, I start him off by asking him to make a list of things that he thinks might be fun. Then over a period of a few weeks he experiments with sampling these different activities. Remember that this is generally a slow process. It takes time for someone to learn how to have a good time, particularly when he has never had any experience doing it.

Over the years, I have had the opportunity to work with many recovering alcoholics who are now alcoholism counselors. One of the first things that I suggest when working with a professional is that he or she make a fun list. Almost always, quite a bit of time has passed since the last experience of these activities. It is also surprising how many counselors include "work" on their list of fun things. This may be true, but if it's all the enjoyment the counselor has going on in his or her life, beware. This counselor could be in for a relapse and a return to active alcoholism.

Why don't you try making a fun list. Right now. Take a pencil and write down three fun things that you love to do, and the date you did each last. If it's been a while since the last time you did EACH of the three things, you might think about taking a vacation. At the least, you might make a determined effort to start reintegrating these things into your life. Having fun is vital to our well-being.

There is a saying that goes, "If you want something done, ask a busy person to do it." A busy person can always find time to do one more thing. I have found this to be true, not only in my own life, but also in the lives of others. Activities seem to creep into our lives and mysteriously multiply.

For this reason, it is important to find out about all of the activities in which you are involved. Many times, when you have a feeling of being overwhelmed by life, there is good reason for feeling overwhelmed — you simply may be doing too much!

Alcoholics, in their first few years of sobriety, have a tendency to become involved in many different activities, and their involvement in these activities sometimes gets out of control. Then they resolve this uncomfortable feeling by adding more activities, which makes their lives feel more out of control. This process goes on and on.

I counseled with a woman who told me she could not seem to relax. She said she felt nervous most of the time and that she was having trouble sleeping. After we had talked for a while, I asked her to make a list of all her activities. Her list looked something like this:

Working a full-time job

Parenting a three-year-old child

Going to five or six A.A. meetings a week

Being involved in a relationship

Sponsoring five new people in A.A.

Volunteering at the local mental health center

Being the secretary of a local civic group

Working in her local community group

Doing volunteer work at the women's center

Exercising at the health spa

Taking evening college classes

This woman was simply amazed to see so many activities in writing. Until she took the time to stop and write her daily experiences in a list, she had no real idea of how full her life had become. One by one, she had added so many activities to her life that she was becoming extremely uncomfortable.

Her next step was to prioritize her involvements and gradually stop doing the things that were least important to her. After she had done this, she calmed down, became less nervous, and stopped having trouble sleeping. She, like many newly-sober people, had difficulty saying no when asked to do things. Now, after making and prioritizing the above list, she no longer felt an obligation to do all that she was asked to do.

I recommend to my clients that they periodically take the time to list all the activities in which they are involved. This activities list is an effective positioning tool to help you become aware of what you are actually doing with your time. This positioning can help to keep you from becoming overwhelmed by activities that creep into your life unnoticed.

Many times a person will have difficulty in prioritizing his list. When this happens, I ask him to imagine that he knows he is going to die in one week. Using this information about his death, I ask him to prioritize his list, placing at the top of the list those activities that are most meaningful to him.

People invariably respond with answers such as, "I would spend more time with my family"; "I would tell my mother I love her"; "I would be kinder to my husband". This method helps the person to focus on what really is of value to him. With this awareness, he can begin to reintegrate into his life those activities that are of real value.

It is important to find out who you relate to, as well as the activities which you enjoy. Who are the significant others in your life? Who are the people you can really talk to?

Many people tell me that they have "lots" of friends that they can talk to, and this may very well be true. These friends, however, are not really part of his life if he does not spend time with them. There is a great deal of difference between having a lot of people to talk to and actually talking to them. Potentially, we can talk to the whole human race. However, this potential is mostly unrealized.

It is important to identify the quality of the conversations that you have with others.

During a counseling session with a client named Tom, I asked him if he had a support group of people that he could talk to. His reply was, "Yes, of course I do." He had his family, his co-workers and the members of his A.A. group. He said that he had plenty of people in his life who he could talk to.

I asked Tom to list six people with whom he felt he could really discuss any major subject, and requested he focus on subjects such as sex, relationship conflicts, employment problems, things that made him feel fearful and guilty, and his day-to-day living problems.

Tom could not come up with six people who he could talk to about these subjects. After some effort, he did come up with two names. When I asked, Tom could not remember when he last had a meaningful conversation with either of these two people.

Tom is typical of someone who easily gets lost in the crowd. He was surrounded by persons with whom he could potentially talk, but he never did, except in safe generalities. By the time Tom came to see me, he was feeling isolated and lonely. He couldn't understand why he felt so alone. His view of himself, that he had a good support group of people with whom he regularly shared, was not substantiated in reality.

At one time, Tom had used his support group, but over the years of his sobriety, he had stopped using them. He became caught up in listening to other people talk to him about their problems, and he slowly stopped talking about himself and his problems. He became unwilling to let people know that he had problems, that he needed to share his feelings.

Listing his support group and dating the last times he had spoken with those on the list was an important process for Tom. By seeing the list, Tom realized that he was living in a fantasy. With the knowledge that he gained from the positioning list, he renewed his commitment to speaking, in depth, to the people in his support system. He also agreed to make an effort to add some new people to his support system.

I suggest my clients ask themselves positioning questions throughout their day. These questions help them to get a position on "right now", so they don't get stuck in a feeling, thought or behavior that will cause them pain. The questions are:

1. What am I feeling right now?

2. What am I thinking about right now?

3. What am I doing right now?

These are important facts to know. Unfortunately, as the movement of the day progresses, most of my clients forget to ask the questions. To bring the positioning questions back into their conscious minds, I ask them to write the questions down and carry them somewhere on their persons, generally some place that they refer to often (with their change, keys or cigarettes, for instance). When they reach for an item and come up with the list of positioning questions, they have the opportunity to stop and take stock of what is going on at that moment in their lives.

The three questions position the client in three of the four dimensions of existence. (The fourth dimension is the all-encompassing dimension of the spirit.) These are:

1. The emotional dimension ("What am I feeling right now?").

2. The mental dimension ("What am I thinking right now?").

3. The physical dimension ("What am I doing right now?").

When a person becomes aware of what he is doing in these three dimensions, he can then change. Awareness is critical. Without the awareness of what is going on with him, the client will remain "stuck", not knowing why he is feeling, thinking or acting the way he is. With awareness can come acceptance. The client can then begin to let go of his painful feelings, irrational thoughts and potentially-damaging behavior.

These positioning statements will help you realize a sense of what is happening in your "here and now". With this realization, you can begin the process of acceptance and change which is a necessary part of growth.

By acquainting ourselves with these simple positioning techniques, we can focus on a clearer picture of what is going on in our lives. Many recovered alcoholics, addicts, and adult children lose their sense of perspective. They get all wrapped up in doing the everyday tasks of living and allow the fun and joy to slip out of their lives. When we can recapture this sense of fun and joy, and learn to live in the present moment, in today, then we truly have been given a gift.

6

Breathing

When a child is born, one of its first acts of independence is to breathe. The child's diaphragm pushes downward and his lungs fill with life-giving air, which is then exhaled (sometimes with a cry). This process of inhalation and exhalation is continued throughout life and is one of the last acts that is taken before death. To breathe is to live.

Most of us know that if we stop breathing for any length of time, death will occur, or the brain will sustain damage that will affect a person's mental and physical faculties. This is common knowledge. What is not common knowledge is that the way that we breathe can have a direct effect on the quality of life that we live.

Our breath is our connection to life. Every minute we breathe approximately 20 times. Although breathing is something that we do constantly, awake or asleep, most of us are unaware of our breathing; we take it for granted. Even now, as you read this, I would guess that there are some who are wondering why I am stating the obvious. They know that breathing is important. What they don't know is that effective breathing can alter the way a person relates to the world.

The alcoholic person has, over the course of his life, learned to breathe in an unhealthy way. If you observe the breath processes, you will notice that most recovering people breathe shallowly and irregularly. This is not surprising. Shallow and uneven breathing is characteristic of the "flight or fight" state of mind and emotions associated with alcoholics.

The alcoholic has spent a number of years in high-stress situations, and his natural stance is always to be on guard, poised, ready to flee or to defend. Active alcoholism forces a person to live this way. Along with other stress symptoms that accompany the flight-or-fight syndrome (i.e., fear, anxiety, rapid heart rate), shallow, uneven breathing is usually present. Over the years this type of breathing becomes a habit to the alcoholic.

Even after the drinking has stopped, this kind of breathing usually continues. The way a person breathes affects his emotional and physical state, and the shallow, rapid breathing of the flight-or-fight syndrome can itself cause anxiety or stress. This cycle will continue over and over. A simple way to break out of this unhealthy cycle is to learn to breathe in a more effective way.

The above is also true for adult children of alcoholics. Due to the high-stress environment of the alcoholic family, the children live with the "flight or fight" syndrome from birth. As one ACoA client of mine reported, "I feel like I've been holding my breath all my life."

Most people breathe by using their chest muscles. Their chests generally rise and fall with their breaths.

Chest breathing is just the opposite of the way babies and children breathe. If you watch a sleeping baby, you can see that his stomach rises and falls with each breathe, not his chest. The child naturally uses his diaphragm to breathe, and diaphragmatic breathing is the most efficient and healthy way to breathe, both for children and adults.

The diaphragm, which is positioned between the lungs and stomach, is the muscle that contracts and relaxes when one is breathing correctly. To determine whether you are breathing diaphragmatically, place one hand below your rib cage, on your stomach. Then take a deep breath. Observe whether your hand moves in or out. Does it move at all? If you are breathing effectively, your hand will move out when you inhale.

Most of the time, your hand either will not move at all, or will move inward when you take a deep breath. This is not surprising, when you consider that most people are taught to hold their stomachs in and their chests out. Unfortunately, this posture inhibits healthy breathing.

You can learn diaphragmatic breathing by placing your hand between the bottom of your rib cage and your navel. As you take a deep breath, push your hand outward with your stomach. As your diaphragm contracts, it will move downward, pushing out the stomach and creating a vacuum in the lungs into which the air rushes. Thus, your hand will move outward when you are breathing diphragmatically.

Diaphragmatic breathing is healthier in part because it increases the circulation of blood in the lower sections of the lungs. When you breathe diaphragmatically, oxygen is drawn down into the lower sections of the lungs and the vital oxygen/carbon dioxide exchange takes place much more efficiently. The person who breathes diaphragmatically provides his body with much more oxygen.

To breathe is both simple and complicated. It is simple because everyone does it all the time. It is as simple as "taking a breath". The breathing process, on the other hand, is complicated: sophisticated biological and chemical exchanges take place during the act of breathing.

And while it is important to breathe deeply and diaphragmatically, it is also important to breathe evenly. Uneven and ragged breathing is a sign of distress. The sob of grief, startled gasp, and the deep, forceful breaths of anger are all signs that a person is in some degree of distress or emotional turmoil. These situations are not necessarily negative, but it is unhealthy to continue to breathe in a shallow, ragged manner after the situation that caused the distress has resolved itself.

Deep breathing is an excellent relaxation method you can use regularly in stressful situations. During the early stages of recovery, many people respond to different kinds of situations with anger, fear, rage and hysteria. Their responses have been pre-programmed into the unconscious, and in many cases the recovering person is as afraid of his response to a situation as he is of the situation itself.

Learning to control breathing during stressful situations will help you to become calmer and more relaxed. This lessening of emotional turmoil will provide you with an opportunity to be able to think and make choices in situations that formerly might have over-whelmed you with fear and anger.

One of my clients became panicked whenever she had to speak in public. Before speaking, her breath would become shallow and ragged, and she would be filled with fear. To help her overcome this, I taught her to use deep breathing before speaking. After doing this a number of times, she became less and less panicked when she spoke in front of a group of people.

As a crisis counselor in the emergency room of a hospital, I used deep breathing with patients many times. When people are frightened and in pain, their breathing becomes shallow and uneven. In order to help these patients deal with their crises (anything from the death of a loved one to free-floating anxiety), I simply helped them to breathe diaphragmatically throughout their crisis phase. I also used this technique myself, whenever I felt my own breathing become stilted or erratic, so I could function as a counselor in a calmer and more effective way.

I use two basic exercises in teaching diaphragmatic breathing.

Exercise One

Sit in an upright position, with back straight. Picture your lungs divided into three parts — a lower, a middle and an upper part. Take a deep, even, continuous breath, and visualize the lower portion of your lungs filling with air, then the middle section of your lungs filling with air, then the upper part of your lungs filling with air. During this breathing process, be aware that as you are breathing into lower lungs, your diaphragm is contracting and is pushing your stomach slightly outward. When the middle section is filling with air, be aware that your chest is expanding slightly. When you are breathing into your upper lungs, be aware that your shoulders are rising slightly. When you exhale, visualize the air leaving the top part of your lungs first, then the middle part, and then the lower part, until all of the air is expelled from your lungs.

When all of the air is expelled from your lungs, become aware of how it feels for the lungs to be empty. Pause for a moment, between exhaling and inhaling, and rest.

Then repeat the process of inhaling and exhaling. Do this for ten cycles of breathing in and out.

Throughout this exercise try to breathe through your nose. Many people are not used to doing this and it may seem uncomfortable at first, but the exercise is most effective when you breathe through the nose.

A variation on the above exercise is to lie on your back and do the same breathing exercise. When doing the exercise in this position, hold your hands on your stomach so you can feel your stomach moving up and down as you breathe. This will help those who have trouble moving their stomachs when they breathe in a sitting or standing position.

When you have practiced doing the above exercise and feel comfortable doing diaphragmatic breathing, it is now appropriate to do this type of breathing at any time during the day, not just when things get stressful. Deep breathing can and should be done 30 to 40 times per day (one deep breath each time). Pick times when deep breathing would be both convenient and beneficial. Some of these occasions might be when you look at the clock, answer the telephone, are stopped at a red light, stalled in traffic, etc. Be creative with your ideas.

Exercise Two

Do the same type of inhalation as in Exercise One, filling your lungs from the lower portion to the upper. When you exhale, exhale completely and sigh audibly while you are exhaling. This is the well-known "sigh of relief". The sigh of relief is effective in letting go of tension and anxiety. At first you may be embarrassed to "sigh" but try doing this exercise at home. It will do wonders to help you relax and let go of tension.

Many recovering people smoke cigarettes. This does not mean that they cannot participate in these breathing exercises. In fact, it is important that they do. Diaphragmatic breathing can assist them in getting much-needed oxygen to parts of the body that are oxygen-deficient because of smoking. If you are a heavy smoker, you may feel a little light-headed during, and for a short period after, the exercise. This is due to the fact that you are not used to getting so much oxygen into your system.

Breathing plays a crucial role in maintaining the integrity of the human organism. We can learn to let go of old habits of shallow breathing and learn to breathe in a healthy way. Breathing, correctly can help generate more vitality and alertness. It can help to relax and let go of stress and tension. To breathe is to live; to breathe fully and deeply is to live fully and deeply. The gift of breath is a gift of life.

7

Bonding
and Intimacy

 Deep within each human being is a desire to become profoundly intimate with another person. This desire to be in a deep union, or bounded in a love/sexual relationship is a healthy and natural aspect of human existence. The love/sexual relationship is an experience that can both enrich and reward the lives of both partners in ways that cannot be imagined, only experienced.

The rewards of this bonded relationship are great. There is a sense of contact and of being connected with another human being in a way that transcends other types of relationships. The risks in this relationship are also great: frustration, confusion and pain can be felt at a depth that hurts to the very core. For many, not having an intimate love relationship means living with a sense of loneliness and isolation that cannot be healed.

It is important at this point to acknowledge that many people who have chosen a single lifestyle find happiness and a fulfilling life. There is a difference, however, between the person who chooses a single lifestyle out of a desire to be single, and the person who chooses a single lifestyle out of frustration and fear of relationships.

Adult children are no different from other people in their desire for a special intimate relationship. The adult child does, however, bring to a relationship a different set of problems that are unique to growing up in an alcoholic or other type of dysfunctional family.

People from dysfunctional families have difficulty with sexual relationships. After taking a close look at the dysfunctional family system, it is easy to see why sexual relationships often are painful and frustrating for adult children. The dysfunctional family operates by four major rules:

1. The Rule of Rigidity
2. The Rule of Silence
3. The Rule of Denial
4. The Rule of Isolation

Every dysfunctional family operates with these rules and every dysfunctional family teaches these rules to the children who grow up in its unhealthy system. Each one of these rules is a barrier to intimacy and each of these rules must be broken, again and again, by the adult child who desires a healthy sexual relationship.* The keyword is "healthy". Many adult children are involved in sexual relationships; unfortunately, these relationships are often

---

*For a more in-depth discussion on the four rules of the alcoholic family see *The Adult Children of Alcoholics Syndrome: From Discovery to Recovery,* by Wayne Kritsberg.

unfulfilling and unhealthy. Many of these relationships either continue, on and on, in a cycle of pain, or end in a painful mess and the adult child goes out and gets into another relationship that ends in the same way. This does not have to happen; the cycle can be broken.

Adult children can learn how to have fulfilling and healthy relationships. It is important for them to understand that a lack of knowledge about how to have a healthy relationship is not a fatal character flaw that cannot be resolved. Adult children learned how to have sexual relationships from their parents. They learned the rules of behavior from their parents. What has been learned can be unlearned. What is not known can be learned. It is never too late for an adult child to learn how to have a healthy relationship.

There is, however, a lot to learn. Adult children need to know, for example, how to communicate honestly about how they feel, the difference between bonding and blending with another, and the difference between solitude and isolation, to name a few. The list of things to learn is impressive and can be overwhelming. It is important for the adult child to keep in mind that everything cannot be learned at once and that learning takes both time and repetition. Even for healthy people, learning the relationship dance is a lifetime process. It is, however, encouraging to experience how quickly a relationship will begin to heal once a commitment to becoming healthy is made, when a couple begins to experiment in relating to each other in new and healthier ways.

Basic to moving toward a healthier relationship is the understanding that in a relationship both partners are equal. There is not one person in the relationship who is either sicker or healthier than the other. Each may have different difficulties in relationships, but this does not mean that one person is at fault. Both partners must share the responsibility for the difficulties and successes of the relationship.

Being involved in a healthy love/sexual relationship is an exciting experience. Essential to this experience is the ability of the partners to bond with each other. The importance of bonding cannot be overstated. Bonding is deep intimate contact with another person which includes the physical expression of deep contact (sex), emotional connections that are experienced at a deep level of trust and openness, and mental connections that include sharing the same basic ideals as your partner. When people bond at a deep level of being, they are making a commitment to share their lives and to acknowledge that their relationship is an integrated part of their spiritual path.

Adult children often have a tendency to confuse bonding with blending. Bonding is the process of deepening the relationship between two people where both the relationship and the individuals in the relationship become stronger and more integrated. Blending, on the other hand, is where each person gets lost in the relationhip and each person tries in various ways to control the other person in order to re-establish his or her own lost individuality. Bonding strengthens both the couple and the individuals; blending weakens both the couple and the individuals.

The following is a bonding exercise for couples who are already in a committed sexual relationship and who wish to deepen that relationship and connect with their partner on deeper and deeper levels of experience. This exercise is most effective when it is repeated many times.

To set the scene for this experience make sure that you will not be disturbed for the next hour. Take the phone off the hook, put out the "do not disturb" sign, make sure the kids are asleep or gone, put out the cat, things like this. Make the room as safe and soft as possible, turn down the lights, perhaps burn some incense. Play some soft meditative music (without words). The exercise produces best results when both partners are not wearing clothing. (So be sure the room is warm enough.) However, since opening and deepening often includes feelings of vulnerability, wearing clothing may feel more comfortable the first few times you do this bonding.

Begin with you and your partner sitting, either on chairs or on the floor, facing each other, close but not touching each other. Do not say anything. Be still.

As you sit looking at each other, become aware of your breathing. Be aware of your breath as it flows in and out of your body. As you become aware of your own natural breathing cycle, also become aware of your partner's breathing cycle. Gradually begin to synchronize your breathing with your partner's. Let your breath come together, both breathing in and out as one.

Make eye contact and hold the eye contact for two or three minutes. Remember that this is a bonding experience, not a contest to see who can stare down the other person. It's OK to blink (eyes need to blink; blinking is healthy). Continue to breathe together.

As you are looking into each other's eyes, become aware of your partner's face. Let your eyes roam freely around your partner's face. Really study your partner's face. Become aware of all parts of the face: the nose, the area around the eyes, the eyelids, the forehead, the mouth, cheeks and hair. Look at the details of your partner's face, the crinkles at the corner of the eyes and mouth, the pores of the skin. Be aware, and love any feature that makes the face unique, such as birthmarks, dimples, perhaps a scar. Really study, really see the face of the one you love. Do this for approximately ten minutes. Remember to continue to breathe together.

One person (it does not matter which one) slowly and gently places the palm of his right hand on the heart of his partner. Then the other person mirrors this action by placing the palm of her right hand on the heart of her partner. Now that you both are touching each other's heart area, place your left hand on your own heart area, over your partner's hand.

The two of you will now be sitting, facing each other, looking at each other, touching each other, and breathing together as one. (It is often helpful to practice the positioning of the hands before you try this bonding experience for the first time).

Now sit in this position for approximately fifteen minutes (it's OK to use a clock). As you are sitting like this, communicate your love to your partner with your eyes and through your hands.

At the end of approximately fifteen minutes, gently disengage your hands. End the experience by saying the affirmation, "I love myself and I love you."

Be still for a few minutes and then share with each other what you experienced during this bonding exercise.

This is often a very powerful experience for both partners. Sometimes the feelings that come up during this experience can be painful and frightening. True bonding with another can be very scary. Do not become discouraged if painful feelings of hurt, anger, fear, shame and guilt come up during this experience. This often happens. Make an agreement with your partner before you begin this exercise that either one of you may end the exercise early if you wish. If the exercise ends early, don't be concerned. You did not do it wrong. Agree to try it again at some future time.

The above experience can produce remarkable results in deepening a relationship. Bonding in a relationship is important. Without a healthy bond, the couple will not experience the deep sense of contact and connectedness that set the special love/sexual relationship apart from other relationships. Still, the exercise is only an exercise. What makes it work is the love and the willingness of the couple to experience and explore new realms of being and sharing. Love and willingness to risk are major keys to deepening intimacy in a relationship.

Adult children often have love and willingness in abundance; what they lack is knowledge — the knowledge of how to effectively use the love and willingness they already possess. Bonding, as well as the other skills necessary to make a healthy relationship work, can be learned. The challenge to the adult child is twofold: first, to learn those skills that are essential to a healthy loving relationship and second, to acknowledge those gifts that they already possess, and to allow those gifts to unfold in a loving and healthy way.

This is truly a gift of love.

8

A
Final Thought

 The gifts discussed in the preceding pages can assist you in looking inside yourself and exploring those inner landscapes of being that exist in each one of us. Discovery of self-love and of self-acceptance are two of the major gifts of this inner journey of self-exploration. These two gifts are essential to the recovery process. Without love and acceptance, there can be no true happiness. We must love and accept ourselves; this is the basis for all of our healthy relationships. I truly believe that we cannot give to others what we do not already possess ourselves. If what we have is fear and self-hatred, that is what we will have to share with others. If we have self-love and self-acceptance, then this is what we will share.

I once asked a very wise man, "Why do we have all of this pain and suffering inside?" He replied, "Someday you will meet a person who is suffering as you have been. You will be able to tell him lovingly that there is hope, that recovery is possible. That, I believe, is reason enough."

Please take the gifts in this book and try them yourselves. I acquired all of the information contained within these pages from others who were willing to share with me. I share these gifts with you, so that you may use them, if you wish, and pass them on to others who are trying to lift themselves from a world of fear, pain and darkness into a place of love, joy, sunlight and recovery.

Reference
Bibliography

Davis, Roy. **An Easy Guide to Meditation.** Georgia: CSA Press, 1978.

Denning, M. and Phillips, O. **The Llewellyn Practical Guide to Creative Visualization.** Minnesota: Llewellyn Publications, 1981.

Fishel, Ruth. **The Journey Within: A Spiritual Path to Recovery.** Florida: Health Communications, 1987.

Gawain, Shakti. **Creative Visualization.** New York: Bantam Books, 1982.

Keating, Thomas. **Open Mind, Open Heart.** Warwick, NY: Amity House, 1986.

Levine, Stephen. **A Gradual Awakening.** New York: Anchor Books, 1979.

Mason, L. **Guide to Stress Reduction.** California: Peace Press, 1979.

Progoff, Ira. **At A Journal Workshop.** New York: Dialogue House Library, 1975.

Ram Dass. **The Journey of Awakening**. New York: Bantam Books, 1978.

Ray, Sondra. **I Deserve Love**. California: Les Femmes Publishing, 1976.

Silverstein, Lee. **Consider the Alternatives**. Minnesota: CompCare Publications, 1977.

Simon, Sidney B.; Howe, Leland W. and Kirschenbaum, Howard. **Values Clarification**. New York: Hart Publishing Company, 1972.

Small, Jacquelyn. **Transformers: The Therapists of the Future**. Florida: Health Communications, 1982.

Smith, Maury. **A Practical Guide to Value Clarification**. California: University Associates, 1977.

Swami Rama; Ballentine, R. and Haymes, A. **Science of Breath**. Pennsylvania: The Himalayan International Institute of Yoga Science and Philosophy, 1979.

Other Books By . . .

HEALTH COMMUNICATIONS, INC.

1721 Blount Road
Pompano Beach, Florida 33069
Phone: 800-851-9100

ADULT CHILDREN OF ALCOHOLICS
Janet Woititz
Over a year on The New York Times Best Seller list,this book is the primer
on Adult Children of Alcoholics.
ISBN 0-932194-15-X   **$6.95**

STRUGGLE FOR INTIMACY
Janet Woititz
Another best seller, this book gives insightful advice on learning to love
more fully.
ISBN 0-932194-25-7   **$6.95**

DAILY AFFIRMATIONS: For Adult Children of Alcoholics
Rokelle Lerner
These positive affirmations for every day of the year paint a mental picture
of your life as you choose it to be.
ISBN 0-932194-27-3   **$6.95**

*CHOICEMAKING: For Co-dependents, Adult Children and Spirituality
Seekers* — Sharon Wegscheider-Cruse
This useful book defines the problems and solves them in a positive way.
ISBN 0-932194-26-5   **$9.95**

LEARNING TO LOVE YOURSELF: Finding Your Self-Worth
Sharon Wegscheider-Cruse
"Self-worth is a choice, not a birthright", says the author as she shows us
how we can choose positive self-esteem.
ISBN 0-932194-39-7   **$7.95**

LET GO AND GROW: Recovery for Adult Children
Robert Ackerman
An in-depth study of the different characteristics of adult children of
alcoholics with guidelines for recovery.
ISBN 0-932194-51-6   **$8.95**

LOST IN THE SHUFFLE: The Co-dependent Reality
Robert Subby
A look at the unreal rules the co-dependent lives by and the way out of the
dis-eased reality.
ISBN 0-932194-45-1   **$8.95**

New Books . . .
from Health Communications

BRADSHAW ON: THE FAMILY: *A Revolutionary Way of Self-Discovery*
John Bradshaw
The host of the nationally televised series of the same name shows us how families can be healed and we as individuals can realize our full potential.
ISBN 0-932194-54-0   **$9.95**

HEALING THE CHILD WITHIN: Discovery and recovery for Adult Children of Dysfunctional Families — Charles Whitfield
Dr. Whitfield defines, describes and discovers how we can reach our Child Within to heal and nurture our woundedness.
ISBN 0-932194-40-0   **$8.95**

WHISKY'S SONG: An Explicit Story of Surviving in an Alcoholic Home
Mitzi Chandler
A beautiful but brutal story of growing up where violence and neglect are everyday occurrences conveys a positive message of survival and love.
ISBN 0-932194-42-7   **$6.95**

New Books on Spiritual Recovery . . .
from Health Communications

THE JOURNEY WITHIN: A Spiritual Path to Recovery
Ruth Fishel
This book will lead you from your dysfunctional beginnings to the place within where renewal occurs.
ISBN 0-932194-41-9   **$8.95**

LEARNING TO LIVE IN THE NOW: 6-Week Personal Plan To Recovery
Ruth Fishel
The author gently introduces you to the valuable healing tools of meditation, positive creative visualization and affirmations.
ISBN 0-932194-62-1   **$7.95**

GENESIS: Spirituality in Recovery for Co-dependents
by Julie D. Bowden and Herbert L. Gravitz
A self-help spiritual program for adult children of trauma, an in-depth look at "turning it over" and "letting go".
ISBN 0-932194-56-7   **$6.95**

GIFTS FOR PERSONAL GROWTH AND RECOVERY
Wayne Kritsberg
Gifts for healing which include journal writing, breathing, positioning and meditation.
ISBN 0-932194-60-5   **$6.95**

Books from . . .
Health Communications

THIRTY-TWO ELEPHANT REMINDERS: A Book of Healthy Rules
Mary M. McKee
Concise advice by 32 wise elephants whose wit and good humor will also
be appearing in a 12-step calendar and greeting cards.
ISBN 0-932194-59-1 $3.95

BREAKING THE CYCLE OF ADDICTION: For Adult Children of Alcoholics
Patricia O'Gorman and Philip Oliver-Diaz
For parents who were raised in addicted families, this guide teaches you
about Breaking the Cycle of Addiction from *your* parents to your children.
Must reading for any parent.
ISBN 0-932194-37-0 $8.95

AFTER THE TEARS: Reclaiming The Personal Losses of Childhood
Jane Middelton-Moz and Lorie Dwinnel
Your lost childhood must be grieved in order for you to recapture your
self-worth and enjoyment of life. This book will show you how.
ISBN 0-932194-36-2 $7.95

ADULT CHILDREN OF ALCOHOLICS SYNDROME: From Discovery to Recovery
Wayne Kritsberg
Through the Family Integration System and foundations for healing the
wounds of an alcoholic-influenced childhood are laid in this important
book.
ISBN 0-932194-30-3 $7.95

OTHERWISE PERFECT: People and Their Problems with Weight
Mary S. Stuart and Lynnzy Orr
This book deals with all the varieties of eating disorders, from anorexia to
obesity, and how to cope sensibly and successfully.
ISBN 0-932194-57-5 $7.95

Orders must be prepaid by check, money order, MasterCard or Visa.
Purchase orders from agencies accepted (attach P.O. documentation)
for billing. Net 30 days.

Minimum shipping/handling — $1.25 for orders less than $25. For
orders over $25, add 5% of total for shipping and handling. Florida
residents add 5% sales tax.

┌─ THE MAGAZINE FOR AND ABOUT . . . ─┐

ADULT CHILDREN
OF ALCOHOLICS

WE UNDERSTAND. . .

. . . what it means to be the child of an alcoholic. We know the confusion, the intense self-criticism, the bottled-up anger you carry with you. You are not alone.

How do we know? Because we, like you, are part of the 28 million Americans who are children of alcoholics. And we have seen our numbers grow into a social movement focused on the special needs and understanding of people like us.

Changes . . . The Magazine For and About Children of Alcoholics, is part of the new vision of hope for CoAs everywhere. The understanding that comes from caring can lead to healing. But none of us can do it alone. We need each other. The isolation, desolation and despair of the alcoholic family is not all that binds us. It is the hope — and the truth — that things will get better.

We hope you share in the vision by subscribing to *Changes* . . . For and About Children of Alcoholics. It's a change for the better.

☐ **YES** . . . Send my subscription to the following address:
☐ 1 Year (6 Issues) . . . $18.00   ☐ 2 Years (12 Issues) . . . $34.00

Your Name: _____

Address: _____

_____

Payment Form (Check One):
☐ Check or Money Order Enclosed (Payable to The U.S. Journal)
☐ M.C. #: _____ Exp. Date: _____
☐ VISA #: _____ Exp. Date: _____
Agency P.O.'s & Vouchers accepted. Attach documentation for billing purposes.

Cardholder's Signature: _____

The U.S. Journal, Inc., 1721 Blount Rd., Suite #1
Pompano Beach, FL 33069 • 1-800-851-9100